CAT BREEDS

MAINE COONS

BY ABBY DOTY

WWW.APEXEDITIONS.COM

Copyright © 2025 by Apex Editions, Mendota Heights, MN 55120. All rights reserved. No part of this book may be reproduced or utilized in any form or by any means without written permission from the publisher.

Apex is distributed by North Star Editions:
sales@northstareditions.com | 888-417-0195

Produced for Apex by Red Line Editorial.

Photographs ©: Shutterstock Images, cover, 1, 4–5, 7, 8–9, 10–11, 12, 13, 15, 16–17, 18, 21, 22–23, 24–25, 26–27, 29; Red Line Editorial, 19

Library of Congress Control Number: 2024943624

ISBN
979-8-89250-311-2 (hardcover)
979-8-89250-349-5 (paperback)
979-8-89250-424-9 (ebook pdf)
979-8-89250-387-7 (hosted ebook)

Printed in the United States of America
Mankato, MN
012025

NOTE TO PARENTS AND EDUCATORS

Apex books are designed to build literacy skills in striving readers. Exciting, high-interest content attracts and holds readers' attention. The text is carefully leveled to allow students to achieve success quickly. Additional features, such as bolded glossary words for difficult terms, help build comprehension.

CHAPTER 1
PLAYTIME 4

CHAPTER 2
BREED HISTORY 10

CHAPTER 3
BIG CATS 16

CHAPTER 4
CAT CARE 22

COMPREHENSION QUESTIONS • 28
GLOSSARY • 30
TO LEARN MORE • 31
ABOUT THE AUTHOR • 31
INDEX • 32

CHAPTER 1

PLAYTIME

A boy plays with his Maine coon in a fenced backyard. The boy throws a ball. His cat chases after it. She brings it back to the boy.

Many Maine coons enjoy playing fetch.

Next, the boy brings out a feather toy. The Maine coon creeps toward him. She sinks low. Then, she pounces and grabs the feathers.

STAYING SAFE

Many Maine coons enjoy being outside. But outdoor areas can be unsafe. Cats can get lost or hurt. Owners should watch their cats carefully when playing outside.

Maine coons tend to be very playful.

Soon, the cat lets go of the toy. She rubs her head against her owner. Then, she runs off to **explore** the yard.

FAST FACT

Unlike many cats, Maine coons enjoy playing in water.

Maine coons sometimes play in sprinklers or fountains.

CHAPTER 2

BREED HISTORY

People don't know the exact **origins** of Maine coons. European ships likely brought long-haired cats across the Atlantic Ocean. By the 1800s, many of these cats lived in America.

Sailors brought cats onto their ships to keep rats and mice away from food.

Maine coons are good hunters. They often catch mice and other small animals.

In America, the cats helped farmers by hunting **rodents**. Over time, the cats' fur became thicker. They also got bigger paws.

COON CATS

Long-haired cats were especially **popular** in the state of Maine. The cats had bushy tails like raccoons. So, people called them coon cats. In the 1860s, Maine farmers began showing their coon cats in fairs.

Thick fur keeps Maine coons warm in winter. Big paws let them walk over snow.

In the early 1900s, Maine coons became an official **breed** in the United States. Later, the cats spread to other countries. Today, many people own Maine coons.

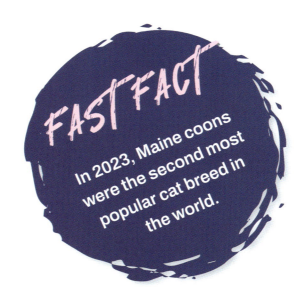

FAST FACT

In 2023, Maine coons were the second most popular cat breed in the world.

Maine coons became the state cat of Maine in 1985.

CHAPTER 3

BIG CATS

Maine coons are the largest breed of house cat. The cats can weigh more than 20 pounds (9 kg). Some grow 40 inches (100 cm) long.

Maine coons take four years to reach their full size.

Maine coons have large, pointy ears.

Maine coons have long fur. Tufts of hair stick out from their toes and ears. The cats also have long, bushy tails.

DOUBLE COATS

A Maine coon's coat has two layers of fur. Both layers are thick and fluffy. The outer layer is **water-resistant**. It helps keep the cat warm and dry.

Maine coons can come in many different fur colors.

Maine coons are active and smart. The cats tend to be easy to train. So, Maine coons often appear in movies and ads.

FAST FACT

Maine coons are quiet cats. They may softly **chirp** or **trill** rather than meow.

Owners can teach Maine coons many tricks.

CHAPTER 4

CAT CARE

Maine coons shed a lot. So, they need regular grooming. Owners should brush their cats at least once a week.

A Maine coon's fur grows thicker during winter. It may need more brushing during this season.

Maine coons also need exercise. Owners should spend at least 10 minutes a day playing with them. Toys and cat furniture help Maine coons stay busy, too.

Owners can get puzzle toys for their cats to play with.

FAST FACT

Maine coons may need extra-large cat furniture and litter boxes.

Maine coons need lots of attention. They do best with owners who spend plenty of time at home. Maine coons prefer not to be alone for very long.

HUNTING AT HOME

Maine coons get along with most people and pets. However, the cats may not be a good fit for homes with small animals. Maine coons might try to hunt birds or rodents.

COMPREHENSION QUESTIONS

Write your answers on a separate piece of paper.

1. Write a few sentences explaining the main ideas of Chapter 3.

2. Would you like to own a Maine coon? Why or why not?

3. How long can a Maine coon grow?
    - A. 10 inches (25 cm)
    - B. 20 inches (51 cm)
    - C. 40 inches (100 cm)

4. Why might Maine coons need extra-large cat furniture and litter boxes?
    - A. Maine coons have bigger bodies than other cats.
    - B. Maine coons need less attention than other cats.
    - C. Maine coons are less active than other cats.

5. What does **pounces** mean in this book?

The Maine coon creeps toward him. She sinks low. Then, she pounces and grabs the feathers.

- **A.** falls off something
- **B.** runs away from something
- **C.** jumps at something

6. What does **grooming** mean in this book?

Maine coons shed a lot. So, they need regular grooming. Owners should brush their cats at least once a week.

- **A.** cleaning and caring for an animal's fur
- **B.** making an animal's fur dirty
- **C.** petting an animal's fur softly

Answer key on page 32.

GLOSSARY

breed

A specific type of cat that has its own look and abilities.

chirp

To make a short, high-pitched sound.

explore

To search or move through an area.

origins

The early parts of something's history.

popular

Liked by or known to many people.

rodents

Small, furry animals with large front teeth, such as rats or mice.

trill

To make a short, high-pitched sound when happy.

water-resistant

Not allowing water to pass through easily.

BOOKS

Clausen-Grace, Nicki. *Maine Coons*. Mankato, MN: Black Rabbit Books, 2020.

Jaycox, Jaclyn. *Read All About Cats*. North Mankato, MN: Capstone Publishing, 2021.

Pearson, Marie. *Cat Behavior*. Minneapolis: Abdo Publishing, 2024.

ONLINE RESOURCES

Visit **www.apexeditions.com** to find links and resources related to this title.

ABOUT THE AUTHOR

Abby Doty is a writer, editor, and booklover from Minnesota.

INDEX

A
active, 20
America, 10, 12
Atlantic Ocean, 10
attention, 27

B
breed, 14, 16

E
exercise, 24

F
farmers, 12–13
fur, 12, 18–19

G
grooming, 22

H
hunting, 12, 27

M
Maine (state), 13

O
origins, 10
owners, 6, 8, 22, 24, 27

Q
quiet, 20

T
training, 20

W
water-resistant, 19

ANSWER KEY:
1. Answers will vary; 2. Answers will vary; 3. C; 4. A; 5. C; 6. A